Dream Tabs

APRIL MCFADDEN

Author Says...

We all have night dreams, day dreams, and dreams to become whatever you want to be. When it comes to night dreams, there are some that are absolutely beautiful, some we don't remember, and some we try to forget.

There are several dream experts and explanations regarding dreams and what they mean.

What do you think they mean?

Numbers 12:6

And he said, "Hear my words: If there is a prophet among you, I the LORD make myself known to him in a vision; I speak with him in a dream."

Date: ___________

Explain Your Dream:

____

____

____

____

____

____

____

Dreams are oftentimes conversations of your deepest thoughts, desires, fears, or messages. What did you do about it?

____

____

____

____

____

Date: _____________

Explain Your Dream:

____

____

____

____

____

____

____

Dreams are oftentimes conversations of your deepest thoughts, desires, fears, or messages. What did you do about it?

____

____

____

____

Date: ___________

Explain Your Dream:

____

____

____

____

____

____

____

Dreams are oftentimes conversations of your deepest thoughts, desires, fears, or messages. What did you do about it?

____

____

____

____

____

Date: ____________

Explain Your Dream:

____

____

____

____

____

____

____

Dreams are oftentimes conversations of your deepest thoughts, desires, fears, or messages. What did you do about it?

____

____

____

____

____

Date: ____________

Explain Your Dream:

____

____

____

____

____

____

____

Dreams are oftentimes conversations of your deepest thoughts, desires, fears, or messages. What did you do about it?

____

____

____

____

Date: _____________

Explain Your Dream:

____

____

____

____

____

____

____

____

Dreams are oftentimes conversations of your deepest thoughts, desires, fears, or messages. What did you do about it?

____

____

____

____

Date: ___________

Explain Your Dream:

____

____

____

____

____

____

____

Dreams are oftentimes conversations of your deepest thoughts, desires, fears, or messages. What did you do about it?

____

____

____

____

Date: _______________

Explain Your Dream:

____

____

____

____

____

____

____

Dreams are oftentimes conversations of your deepest thoughts, desires, fears, or messages. What did you do about it?

____

____

____

____

____

Date: ____________

Explain Your Dream:

____

____

____

____

____

____

____

Dreams are oftentimes conversations of your deepest thoughts, desires, fears, or messages. What did you do about it?

____

____

____

____

Date: _____________

Explain Your Dream:

____

____

____

____

____

____

____

____

Dreams are oftentimes conversations of your deepest thoughts, desires, fears, or messages. What did you do about it?

____

____

____

____

Date: _____________

Explain Your Dream:

____

____

____

____

____

____

____

Dreams are oftentimes conversations of your deepest thoughts, desires, fears, or messages. What did you do about it?

____

____

____

____

____

Date: _______________

Explain Your Dream:

____

____

____

____

____

____

____

Dreams are oftentimes conversations of your deepest thoughts, desires, fears, or messages. What did you do about it?

____

____

____

____

____

Date: _______________

Explain Your Dream:

____

____

____

____

____

____

____

Dreams are oftentimes conversations of your deepest thoughts, desires, fears, or messages. What did you do about it?

____

____

____

____

____

Date: _______________

Explain Your Dream:

____

____

____

____

____

____

____

____

Dreams are oftentimes conversations of your deepest thoughts, desires, fears, or messages. What did you do about it?

____

____

____

____

Date: ___________

Explain Your Dream:

____

____

____

____

____

____

____

Dreams are oftentimes conversations of your deepest thoughts, desires, fears, or messages. What did you do about it?

____

____

____

____

____

Date: _____________

Explain Your Dream:

____

____

____

____

____

____

____

____

Dreams are oftentimes conversations of your deepest thoughts, desires, fears, or messages. What did you do about it?

____

____

____

____

Date: _____________

Explain Your Dream:

____

____

____

____

____

____

____

____

Dreams are oftentimes conversations of your deepest thoughts, desires, fears, or messages. What did you do about it?

____

____

____

____

____

Date: ________________

Explain Your Dream:

____

____

____

____

____

____

____

Dreams are oftentimes conversations of your deepest thoughts, desires, fears, or messages. What did you do about it?

____

____

____

____

____

Date: _____________

Explain Your Dream:

____

____

____

____

____

____

____

Dreams are oftentimes conversations of your deepest thoughts, desires, fears, or messages. What did you do about it?

____

____

____

____

____

Date: _______________

Explain Your Dream:

____

____

____

____

____

____

____

Dreams are oftentimes conversations of your deepest thoughts, desires, fears, or messages. What did you do about it?

____

____

____

____

____

Date: ____________

Explain Your Dream:

____

____

____

____

____

____

____

Dreams are oftentimes conversations of your deepest thoughts, desires, fears, or messages. What did you do about it?

____

____

____

____

Date: ___________

Explain Your Dream:

____

____

____

____

____

____

____

Dreams are oftentimes conversations of your deepest thoughts, desires, fears, or messages. What did you do about it?

____

____

____

____

____

Date: _____________

Explain Your Dream:

____

____

____

____

____

____

____

____

Dreams are oftentimes conversations of your deepest thoughts, desires, fears, or messages. What did you do about it?

____

____

____

____

Date: _______________

Explain Your Dream:

____

____

____

____

____

____

____

____

Dreams are oftentimes conversations of your deepest thoughts, desires, fears, or messages. What did you do about it?

____

____

____

____

Date: _______________

Explain Your Dream:

____

____

____

____

____

____

____

Dreams are oftentimes conversations of your deepest thoughts, desires, fears, or messages. What did you do about it?

____

____

____

____

____

Date: _____________

Explain Your Dream:

____

____

____

____

____

____

____

____

Dreams are oftentimes conversations of your deepest thoughts, desires, fears, or messages. What did you do about it?

____

____

____

____

Date: ____________

Explain Your Dream:

____

____

____

____

____

____

____

Dreams are oftentimes conversations of your deepest thoughts, desires, fears, or messages. What did you do about it?

____

____

____

____

____

Date: _____________

Explain Your Dream:

____

____

____

____

____

____

____

Dreams are oftentimes conversations of your deepest thoughts, desires, fears, or messages. What did you do about it?

____

____

____

____

Date: _____________

Explain Your Dream:

____

____

____

____

____

____

____

Dreams are oftentimes conversations of your deepest thoughts, desires, fears, or messages. What did you do about it?

____

____

____

____

____

Date: _____________

Explain Your Dream:

____

____

____

____

____

____

____

Dreams are oftentimes conversations of your deepest thoughts, desires, fears, or messages. What did you do about it?

____

____

____

____

I had more of these dreams!

Congratulations!

You dedicated 30 days of your life to try to understand your dreams!.

After these 30 days, you should be able to see what the majority of your dreams are, get close to understanding what is causing them, and release forms of anxiety and tension. Your dreams will continue so get another journal so that you can keep tabs on them..

Joel 2:28

"And it shall come to pass afterward, that I will pour out my Spirit on all flesh; your sons and your daughters shall prophesy, your old men shall dream dreams, and your young men shall see visions."

April McFadden

About the Author

Growing up in a small town helped April with how she communicates with others. She learned that oftentimes than not, people just need that personal connection when accepting advice from others. April is always trying to find a way to reach the masses with her tips that she has developed over the years and ways to encourage others .

April has such a love for family. She has been with her husband for 20 years with 14 of those years being married. They share a beautiful daughter who has big dreams of her own. She is the sole owner of Abby Red Accessories and is known on social media as Abby Red in which she uses her platform to encourage her followers to be grateful and how to look good doing it!

April has made it her mission to keep her family, friends, and followers in the forefront of her life's journey.